Self-Esteem:
A Passport for Life

PARENTING

Self-Esteem: A Passport for Life

Germain Duclos

160201

Éditions de l'Hôpital Sainte-Justine

Mother and Child University Hospital Centre

Canadian Cataloguing in Publication Data

Duclos, Germain

   Self-esteem: a passport for life

   (Parenting)
   Translation of: L'estime de soi, un passeport pour la vie.
   Includes bibliographical references.

   ISBN 2-921858-93-2

   1. Self-esteem in children. 2. Child psychology. 3. Child rearing. 4. Parent and child. I. Hôpital Sainte-Justine. II. Title. III. Series: Parenting (Montréal, Quebec).

BF723.S3D8213 2001   155.4'182   C00-942106-8

Translation: Carolyn Bastable

Cover Page Illustration: Courtesy of Pauline Paquin
                        Sainte-Adèle, Quebec

Computer Graphics: Céline Forget

Publications Service, Hôpital Sainte-Justine
3175, chemin de la Côte-Sainte-Catherine
Montreal, Quebec H3T 1C5
Telephone: (514) 345-4671
Fax: (514) 345-4631

Legal Deposit: Bibliothèque nationale du Québec, 2001
National Library of Canada, 2001

Acknowledgements

▼

This book is dedicated to psychoeducators Thérèse Dubois-Costopoulos and Marcel Lapointe, for guiding me in the right professional direction.

I would also like to express thanks to the following people who helped with the production of this book:

Luc Bégin, for his tremendous patience throughout this project.

Sylvie Bourcier, for her unflagging support.

Lucie Brodeur, for always being there.

Johanne Ménard, for her enthusiasm and original ideas.

Ginette Choinière, for the care she took in revising this work.

Claire Chabot and Sylvie Payette, for their dedication to children.

Martin Duclos, psychoeducator, who revised the theoretical content of the translation.

TABLE OF CONTENTS

▼

Introduction

▼

Self-esteem is becoming an increasingly important issue in the field of education and mental health. It is also being discussed on a regular basis in the media. Why the sudden interest? Is it just another passing fad, or does it denote a deeper trend of thought, capable of changing our attitudes as individuals, parents or teachers?

Anyone who works in the field of human relations knows that self-esteem is one of the main factors involved in human development. It forms the basis of a person's upbringing and essentially guides children and teenagers through their emotional, social, intellectual and moral lives.

Many parents have questions about the attitudes and methods most likely to guarantee that their children will develop properly. These questions are often of deep concern, because of the climate of insecurity that is prevalent in the family circle and our economy today. We must not forget that we live in a constantly changing society, one that questions many values and offers very few stable reference models or activities upon which we can firmly rely.

The development of self-esteem is a continuous process and an integral part of our children's upbringing. This process must draw on sound methods and, above all, appropriate educational attitudes. Self-esteem flourishes when parents and teachers display a warm attitude toward children, afford them the attention they require, regularly emphasize positive actions, believe in children's ability to overcome challenges and avoid hurtful words and sarcastic tones.

This book is intended for adults responsible for raising children and for those who are looking to acquire the appropriate attitudes and methods for guiding children toward independence and hope in the future. It analyzes current theoretical and practical knowledge as applied to the development of self-esteem in children.

Chapter 1 discusses self-esteem in general, provides a definition of the concept and describes its development and intrinsic characteristics. Chapter 2 mainly deals with confidence, the basic component of self-esteem. Self-knowledge is the focus of chapter 3, the sense of belonging to a group is the highlight of chapter 4, and competency is discussed in the fifth and final chapter of the book. Confidence, self-knowledge, the sense of belonging to a group and competency all contribute to building the self-esteem that will serve as a child's passport for life. Each chapter also proposes strategies and practical advices on how to help children experience these feelings.

Research clearly demonstrates that self-esteem helps prevent all kinds of behavioural and learning problems, as well as safeguarding against depression. Self-esteem is built on close and harmonious relationships that enable us to confidently overcome difficulties in life. As children grow up, they are able to foster self-esteem in others because they can rely on their own self-esteem. Self-esteem is the most precious gift that can be passed from one generation to another.

CHAPTER 1

DEFINITION AND CHARACTERISTICS OF SELF-ESTEEM

▼

Today we hear a lot of talk about self-esteem, so much so, that the word is becoming a part of everyday speech. Consequently, it is easy to confuse self-esteem with confidence, self-assurance and determination.

Every human being creates their own idea of themselves and develops a self-image that varies considerably over time, based on their personal experiences. Recent research has shown that this self-portrait changes throughout a person's life, and continues even past 80.

A Definition of Self-Esteem

Dictionaries generally define self-esteem as a favorable feeling that stems from a good opinion of one's self-worth and value. The *Dictionnaire actuel de l'éducation** speaks of self-esteem as the value that one places upon oneself as a whole, and adds that self-esteem draws upon a person's basic confidence in their ability and self-worth.

For our part, we consider that self-esteem is the *consciousness of self-worth* that we recognize in ourselves with respect to

---

* Legendre, Reynald. *Dictionnaire actuel de l'éducation*. Montreal: Guérin éditeur, Paris: Éditions Eska, 1993.

different areas. In a manner of speaking, it is a set of attitudes and beliefs that enables us to face reality and the world.

It is important to clarify what we mean by *consciousness of self-worth*. The issue is not self-worth per se, but the consciousness of it. There are many people (children, teenagers and adults) who demonstrate remarkable qualities, competency and talent but, because they are not conscious of these traits, they still have a low esteem of themselves. Being in command of our particular strengths and skills does not necessarily mean that we have a healthy self-esteem. The key to self-esteem lies in process of raising consciousness. Self-esteem is made up of the emotional representation that we have of ourselves in relation to our qualities and skills, and our ability to store this image in our memory so that it may be put to use to overcome difficulties, confront challenges and face the future with hope.

Self-esteem is not at all synonymous with narcissism, nor is it a feeling of self-admiration associated with egocentricity, self-aggrandizement or omnipotence. Self-esteem is the awareness of one's personal difficulties and limitations. People with high self-esteem are able to say, "I have qualities, strengths and talents that give me personal worth, even though I face difficulties and know my limitations." Unfortunately, in our Judeo-Christian society, self-esteem is far too often associated with vanity, pride and egotism.

Consequently, self-esteem implies that we have a realistic perception of ourselves. This changes and improves as we go through life and our personality develops.

Self-esteem is the overall positive value that we recognize in ourselves as individuals and in each important aspect of our lives. We can have a healthy self-esteem as employees, but a very negative self-image as parents or lovers.

Some authors feel that we often confuse the self-esteem related to a person's makeup (or a person's intrinsic value) with the self-esteem related to a person's actions, appearance or performance (how a person seems to be).* Unfortunately, many people judge themselves solely on their performance, physical appearance or reputation. Their self-esteem therefore depends on the approval and judgement of others. These people come to experience performance anxiety or a pressing need to do well in order to be appreciated and loved. The value that they attribute to themselves is mainly extrinsic and often inconsistent, because it depends on approval over which they have no control.

We must not forget that other people's opinions are based on the regard that we have for ourselves. Children or adults with a healthy self-esteem have more confidence in their abilities and demonstrate more determination in achieving their objectives. This kind of attitude will result in others having a positive opinion of them. This is known as the dynamic cycle of the mutually beneficial relationship between "what *really* is" and "what *seems* to be."

Lastly, we must emphasize that everyone, especially children, will feel liked if they have a quality relationship with people who are important in their lives. With this type of relationship, children will be able to appreciate their own qualities and personal characteristics, separately from their appearance or performance. Love and confidence represent the psychological nourishment that a person draws upon for the energy needed in life. We are in harmony with ourselves and feel happy when there is consistency between "who we

* Monbourquette, Jean, Myrna Ladouceur and Jacqueline Desjardins-Proulx. *Je suis aimable, je suis capable: parcours pour l'estime de l'affirmation de soi.* Outremont, Quebec: Novalis, 1998. p. 4.

really are" and "who we *seem* to be," and when we are aware of the positive value of these two dimensions of our inner makeup.

At the Root of Self-Esteem

What is the prime source of self-esteem? Many studies maintain that self-esteem stems from a close relationship. Everyone who has felt loved in the past or who still feels loved (even if by only one person) can tell themselves that they are loveable and that they have self-worth.

We are not born with an already formed self-image. Children first learn to recognize themselves in the eyes of the people who are important to them such as their parents, brothers, sisters, teachers and, finally, their friends.

This period of bonding is fundamental to the psychological growth of every human being. It forms the basis of self-esteem. The initial feeling of self-worth is further enriched by positive feedback from the people who are involved in children's lives, emphasizing their strengths, qualities and successes.

As infants, children realize that adults respond to their cries and pamper them with love and affection. This creates an inner feeling of importance. When, at 2 years of age, children oppose the people around them and recognize that they are allowed to make choices, they develop an inner feeling of being "capable." Around age 4, when they strut around with a "look how good I am" attitude and are recognized as sons or daughters, children develop an inner feeling of being important enough to have a place in life. At 6 years of age, when children's learning becomes more intellectual and their skills are praised, they develop an inner feeling of being competent.

Self-esteem can temporarily change, increase or decrease throughout life as the result of a whole range of experiences. Changes that occur during the various stages of life become part of the continuity of self, giving a feeling of unity and inner coherence.

A Cyclical and Ever-Changing Phenomenon

Self-esteem can develop at any age and changes according to the stage of life at that particular time. The first few years of life, however, are of great importance because they represent our psychological foundation, so to speak. However, this does not infer that other stages of life are not filled with challenges.

The consciousness of self-worth is therefore cyclical and ever-changing. To illustrate this point, let us consider the following situation: a man, who has a healthy self-esteem due to the strong relationships he has with the people around him, who likes his job which makes him feel valued, and is involved in many activities, suddenly experiences a setback. This setback — an illness, loss of employment or separation — temporarily affects his self-esteem. But the man is able to deal with his difficulties and adapt because of the embedded, positive perception that he has of himself. Being aware of his resources and personal strengths, he is able to use these to resolve his problems.

Our self-esteem is enriched by our experiences in life. When we are aware of our abilities and know how to utilize our personal resources, we can create adaptive mechanisms to help us manage stress and overcome difficulties. Our self-esteem increases with the personal awareness and satisfaction we feel when we surmount a formidable challenge, and gives us hope for the future. Self-esteem is the awareness we acquire over time of our self-worth, strengths, qualities and skills that enable us to live in harmony with ourselves and others. It is a conscious supply of the strengths that help us overcome obstacles and manage stress in our lives. It is in this respect that self-esteem is a passport for life.

Quality Relationships

Children's self-esteem is influenced by the close relationships they develop with adults who are important in their lives. Favourable remarks from these adults contribute greatly to the development of a healthy self-esteem. On the other hand, negative comments or judgements can destroy children's self-image. Closeness, therefore, is clearly a double-edged sword.

How much effect an adult's positive or negative comments have on children depends on how important the adult is in their lives. Children's self-esteem is significantly influenced by the quality of their interaction with adults. Self-esteem is that little sparkle children have in their eyes when they feel proud. But this spark can flicker and even be extinguished by sarcasm and criticism.

Children do not magically develop a healthy self-esteem because they have small successes. It takes a lot more for them to see themselves in a positive, stable light. This is where adults come into play. Their role is to emphasize children's positive behaviours and achievements so that they will become etched in the children's minds. Without positive feedback, children cannot realize what they have achieved or commit it to memory. Adults must regularly revitalize children's recollection of past achievements in order for these memories to remain in their minds. Self-esteem functions and thrives on memory.

If newly acquired information or skills are not refreshed on a regular basis, they will be quickly forgotten. It is up to adults to stir children's memories and help them talk about their positive actions and achievements. This is how good behaviour and accomplishments become embedded in a child's psyche. Bringing out positive memories can be done in many different ways such as conversation, writing, drawing, photos, etc.

Developing Self-Esteem

We now understand more clearly how self-esteem is developed in children. Firstly, it depends on the positive feedback children receive from the people they consider important in their lives. By emphasizing the child's achievements, these people confirm his/her worth. Therefore, children's self-esteem is derived from external sources. Over time, as children continue to receive positive feedback, their self-esteem becomes internalized and is fed by their inner thoughts — i.e. the positive or negative conversation they hold with themselves inside their heads.

To assess the quality of our own self-esteem, we must become aware of the opinions we have of ourselves during our inner conversations. Positive opinions boost our self-esteem. However, when setbacks or failures occur, our self-esteem can be shaken until our inner thoughts become positive again and revitalize it.

Some authors feel that the quality of a person's self-esteem can be assessed by measuring the following three items:*

- A person's view of themselves (who they *really* are on the inside) and their actions (who they *seem* to be on the outside). *How they see themselves.*

- A person's inner conversation about themselves and their performance. *How they hear themselves.*

---

* Monbourquette, Ladouceur and Desjardins-Proulx, op. cit.

- A person's feelings about themselves and their actions. *How much they like themselves.*

We cannot expect children to achieve such a systematic evaluation of the quality of their self-esteem. However, children who have reached the age of 7 or 8 can get to know themselves better with the help of the adults who are active participants in their lives. These adults can assist children in developing a more critical and objective opinion about themselves as well as activate their inner thoughts. The internal conversations enable children to listen to how they feel about themselves and their performance, helping them better appreciate their intrinsic value.

True self-esteem does not really exist until children reach 7 or 8. Preschool children's intellectual skills have not developed enough to exercise self-criticism and conduct a true inner conversation. Children between the ages of 3 and 6 still have innocent, magical perceptions of themselves. They cannot analyze their past actions on a sequential, causal or logical level.

Preschool children's thoughts are too self-centered for them to have a good consciousness of themselves. However, this age group has already developed a self-image based on the very recent past. The concept of self in these very young children is restricted to what has just happened; they are limited to the recent past and a specific spatial framework. The concept of self prepares them for the advent of self-esteem.

With the appearance of logical thought processes around the age of 7 or 8, children are able to draw on positive self-perceptions arising from past experience and integrate them into their self-esteem. This explains why it is so important to express positive attitudes toward preschool children, so that, when they reach 7 or 8, they will have healthy self-esteem. When children begin to self-criticize themselves (around the same age), they are greatly affected by their verbal or internal self-assessment of their abilities in the areas important to those who have a significant impact on their lives. Children of this age are capable of determining their self-worth overall and in each aspect of their lives, based on their personal criteria or those of the adults important to them. Children begin to assess their self-worth and outwardly express their self-esteem toward others through their behaviour, speech and attitudes.

Learning from Mistakes and Failures

Our self-esteem is nourished by our accomplishments in our daily lives. Self-esteem cannot flourish or develop in an environment of repeated failure. Nevertheless, we must all learn from failure, and use the knowledge we acquire to reassure us about our self-worth. However, the memory of our failures will almost always remain present in our minds.

Mistakes could be said to be a source of realization and personal growth. They enable us to adjust or change our ideas and actions when pursuing a goal. Mistakes allow changes to be made, and must not be confused with failure. They are part of the normal learning process, while failure is a negative outcome, the unsuccessful attempt to achieve a learning objective.

Experiencing Success

Reaching learning goals is always invigorating and helps boost our self-esteem. The perception of success, however, varies from one person to the next. It is mostly subjective, in that it stems from our expectations, ambitions, values and level of perfectionism.

Two groups of people, in particular, have greater difficulty maintaining a healthy level of self-esteem. The first group consists of children, teenagers and adults who regularly experience failure and are frequently dissatisfied with themselves. The second group includes over-ambitious people and perfectionists who undervalue the importance of the goals they have achieved. Their ambitions are set too high and consequently will never be reached. Perfectionists refuse to accept any form of mistake and everything they involve themselves in must be done to perfection. These highly demanding people rarely enjoy their successes and are often dissatisfied with themselves.

Our self-esteem is high when we succeed at doing things that meet or exceed our ambitions. Success makes us feel proud, efficient and competent, and further strengthens how we feel about ourselves. In order for children to experience success, they must be given realistic objectives and be confident about achieving them. Realistic goals help protect self-esteem.

It has been clearly established that self-esteem is the basis for motivation. This explains why children cannot aspire to reach their goals or achieve success if they are not cognizant of their own self-worth. In other words, children must rely on their memory of past successes to continue being successful. Their recollection of past success allows them to realistically anticipate the possibility of future success. But they only remember their accomplishments if adults have emphasized them as they occur. Adults must also regularly reactivate positive memories when introducing children to new challenges and learning experiences. Children draw upon these memories for the energy and hope needed to persevere with what they are doing. Being successful brings children a feeling of personal pride, further increasing their self-esteem. This is the dynamic learning cycle, of which self-esteem is the main building block.

Variations in Self-Esteem

Everyone's self-esteem fluctuates in a vertical fashion. It is not the same at 20 years of age as it is at 40. It also changes on a horizontal scale. Since self-esteem is not narcissism, it is difficult to believe that people can have strong self-esteem in every aspect of their lives. No one is equally motivated or competent in everything they do. Our feelings of self-worth vary with the areas of activity (e.g. physical, social, artistic, scholastic, etc.). The same holds true for children: their motivation fluctuates according to the activity they are involved in at a given time. For instance, children may have a high self-esteem with regard to physical activities because they feel competent, yet have a lower self-esteem in social situations because they feel awkward interacting with people. Children's development curves follow an up-and-down pattern, and each child has his own individual pace of development. This applies to everyone, which is why self-esteem is described as having a disharmonious profile.

Self-esteem evolves as a continuous, integrated process that marks all phases of development. In addition to the needs and challenges associated with each phase, learning, whether simple or complex, has a significant impact on this process. The road to self-esteem is therefore a dynamic, integral part of growing up, at times forging ahead, at others faltering. Like life, self-esteem is cyclical, sometimes unstable, always changing.

A Precious Gift

It is important to view self-esteem in terms of development. If we refer to Abraham Maslow's pyramid of universal needs, self-esteem is placed fourth in the hierarchy of needs.*

---

* Maslow, Abraham H. *Toward a Psychology of Being.* 3rd ed. New York, John Wiley & Sons, 1998. 320 p.

On the first level of this pyramid are the basic needs of survival (e.g. decent food, shelter and clothing). These essential needs must be satisfied before adults can help children develop self-esteem. The second level in the pyramid is ensuring that children are provided with a safe physical and psychological living environment, one that promotes an attitude of confidence with regard to themselves and others.

Close, stable and loving relationships with people who are important in children's lives form the third level. These relationships provide, in a manner of speaking, the psychological nourishment that every individual requires. Consequently, adults must make sure that children interact with family and friends so that they experience feelings of belonging to a group. Children are unable to develop self-esteem until these three levels of needs are satisfied, at least to a large extent. Without the proper satisfaction of the essentials (necessities for survival, safe physical and psychological surroundings and close loving relationships with others), any attempt to develop self-esteem will have uncertain results or simply prove futile.

Nevertheless, self-esteem can develop at any age. Consequently, promoting the creation of a positive self-image in children is essential, as is preparing these youngsters to be aware of their own self-worth. By fostering healthy self-esteem in children, we can safeguard them against adjustment and learning disabilities and enhance their whole life.

If children see that the people around them view them as important, valued individuals, they will gradually cultivate a positive self-image, begin to like who they are and feel proud of themselves. Later in life, children will be able to draw on this precious gift for the hope and courage to overcome the difficulties they are bound to encounter.

As we have seen, self-esteem is the process of recognizing skills used in adjusting to and managing the inevitable pressures of life. By being aware of our strengths, we allow ourselves to dream, set realistic goals and look to the future with hope.

The Components of Self-Esteem

In the Introduction to this book, the following four elements of self-esteem were mentioned: confidence, self-knowledge, the sense of belonging to a group and competency. Confidence is a prerequisite for self-esteem. People must first feel confident in their lives, so that they can acquire new knowledge and thus enhance their self-esteem. The other three components of self-esteem function differently. Self-knowledge, the sense of belonging to a group and competency are all stimulated by employing appropriate educational attitudes and sound methods at every stage of development and every period in life. Security and confidence are therefore of great significance. We will discuss the four elements of self-esteem in more detail further on in this book.

Self-Esteem, Liking Oneself and Self-Assurance

What is the correlation between *self-esteem* and *liking oneself*? The latter can be defined as a strong feeling of self-worth and dignity, which means that people may feel hurt if they are underestimated and want others to hold them in high regard. The two terms are obviously closely related and their distinction lies in the concept that esteem and *liking* generate in our minds.

It is important to note that we can have esteem for someone without necessarily liking them. We can recognize a person's qualities and skills beyond their immediate environment (e.g. a public or political figure) without actually liking them as an individual. However, the opposite is not true: we cannot like a person if we do not have esteem for them — i.e. we do not recognize their personal and intrinsic value. In a close, loving relationship, it is important that we appreciate, admire and value the other person's skills and attitudes.

By comparing *liking oneself* with *self-esteem*, we can understand that it is impossible for people to like themselves if they do not esteem themselves — that is, they fail to acknowledge their self-worth. As we saw earlier, an awareness of self-worth first stems from the feeling of being appreciated and liked because of our personal attributes (qualities, strengths, behaviour and unique identity).

Some authors feel that there is a functional link of continuity between *self-esteem* and *self-assurance*. These writers believe that self-esteem is derived from the mental picture we have of ourselves, whereas self-assurance is the outward expression of these mental pictures.* For children, in particular, these mental pictures first depend upon positive feedback from the people they are close to and, later, are nourished by positive inner conversations related to their self-image. These same authors consider that people with high self-esteem will be more aware of their own dignity. They will have a definite appreciation of themselves in all aspects of their lives and will consequently command the respect of others. They will take more intellectual risks, strive to accomplish projects and follow them through to completion. People who are passive, inhibited or consider themselves victims of events will not be respected by others or be able to assert themselves because of their low self-esteem and subconscious psychological blocks.

It is important to understand that self-assertiveness is expressed in various ways (speech, writing, physical and intellectual activity, body language, art, etc.) based on the person's identity and individual style. In short, a person's self-assurance is the extension and outward demonstration of that person's self-esteem. Self-assurance is, in a way, self-esteem communicated through action.

---

* Monbourquette, Ladouceur and Desjardins-Proulx, op. cit.

Attitudes and Skills of Children with a Positive Self-Image

Children with a positive self-image can demonstrate the following attitudes and skills:

- Feel secure and relaxed
- Have a general sense of well-being
- Feel confident in front of adults
- Remember their successes
- Recognize their qualities and skills
- Feel confident in their own abilities
- Confront new situations
- Are motivated by new challenges and learning experiences
- Persevere when faced with difficulty
- Perceive their differences
- Perceive and accept differences in others
- Command the respect of others
- Demonstrate self-assurance and independence
- Show initiative
- Demonstrate imagination and creativity
- Find peaceful solutions to social conflicts
- Cooperate with others
- Feel comfortable in a group

These feelings, attitudes and skills cannot all be experienced at the same time. However, by encouraging a healthy self-esteem, children will be able to experience these feelings and incorporate these attitudes and skills into their daily lives.

Positive and Negative Parental Attitudes Regarding Children's Self-Esteem

Positive Attitudes	Negative Attitudes
Demonstrate a warm attitude toward children	Fail to be around children Fail to provide a stable psychological environment
Be reliable in meeting children's needs	Fail to respond to children's needs
Express unconditional love	Have unrealistic expectations
Emphasize and praise success	Ignore children's achievements or regard them as unimportant
Highlight children's difficulties, while sparing their pride and providing means for improvement	Blame children for their inadequacies
Provide children with a stable lifestyle, with respect to time and space	Fail to provide a consistent lifestyle
Set clear, reassuring rules of conduct	Be too strict or too permissive
Be consistent when enforcing rules of conduct	Constantly change attitudes regarding rules of conduct

Positive Attitudes	Negative Attitudes
Remain firm on important values, yet be flexible on other issues	Be too strict or too permissive
Impose logical, natural correction when misbehaviour occurs	Impose harsh or irrelevant correction when misbehaviour or ignore altogether
Reduce children's stress by preparing them for change, minimizing the number of stress factors in their lives, and helping them find ways of calming down when stressed	Show obvious signs of stress; overestimate children's ability to adjust
Demonstrate trustworthiness	Fail to display a welcoming attitude and ready availability toward children
Trigger children's memories of past accomplishments	Ignore children's achievements or regard them as unimportant
Highlight children's strengths	Emphasize children's difficulties rather than their strengths
Provide support when children face difficulty	Overprotect children

Positive Attitudes	Negative Attitudes
Encourage children to find solutions to their problems	Solve problems for children
Use positive language that enhances their self-worth	Use hurtful language toward children; humiliate them, use sarcasm
Encourage the expression of feelings and emotions	Discourage the expression of feelings or needs, or dismiss them
Display openness toward others	Have too much control over children's social interactions
Encourage unselfish and cooperative behaviour	Instill individualism and a sense of competition
Encourage children to make friends and manage disputes on their own	Resolve children's disputes for them
Delegate appropriate responsibilities	Have expectations that are too high or too low
Encourage children to make choices and develop their independence	Maintain children's dependence and exert excessive control
Promote creativity	Ignore or fail to value children's creativity

Positive Attitudes	Negative Attitudes
Emphasize initiative	Ignore or fail to emphasize children's initiative
Respect children's motivation	Impose parents' motivation
Respect children's pace of development	Force children to learn too quickly
Emphasize the learning process rather than results	Focus solely on results
Acknowledge that mistakes can occur	Impose perfectionist viewpoints and blame children for their mistakes
Dedramatize mistakes	Impose perfectionism on children
Play and have fun with children	Fail to be available for children; engage only in activities that focus on performance or competition

CHAPTER 2

FOSTERING A SENSE OF CONFIDENCE

▼

Feelings of confidence are the basic prerequisites to self-esteem. They are essential to learning and experiencing important things in life.

Satisfying the Need for Security

Children first develop feelings of confidence from the close relationship they have with their parents, which makes them feel secure.

All parents know that children need to feel they live in a physically safe environment. This is their first concern when choosing educational facilities for their children (daycare centre, school, etc.). They want to ensure that there is sufficient supervision and no risk of physical injury or sickness. They instinctively want to guarantee their child's physical safety. However, parents may not attribute the same degree of importance to their children's psychological security. Yet, this type of security is equally essential to the children's developmental process. When parents afford constant care to their children and are active participants in their lives, children slowly develop a sense of psychological security, which will gradually become transformed into feelings of confidence.

While they may express it differently, adults also need to feel secure. Some do not enjoy their work, but continue to do it because of a need for security. Others may strongly desire a permanent job and agree to give up their real dreams and ambitions to satisfy their need for security.

Adults who are themselves insecure will have difficulty making their children feel secure. Parents and teachers must first learn to be confident and manage their own stress if they want children to be confident. Security and insecurity are both highly contagious!

The main role of any parent or teacher is to adequately respond to children's developmental needs (i.e. survival, security, love, closeness, self-assurance, independence, learning, etc.). When parents fail to satisfy these needs, children suffer from neglect and their development and future are jeopardized.

It is important not to confuse *needs* with *desires*. Children who want to be loved and stimulated are expressing a need. On the other hand, children who ask for their own television for their room are expressing a desire. Parents who fulfill almost all of their children's desires as if they were needs will have thoroughly spoiled children who will become impossible to satisfy.

To protect their children, parents must adopt attitudes about their upbringing and provide living conditions in line with their children's developmental needs. Parents who do not take on this responsibility are guilty of negligence. However, overprotecting children or not allowing them to do things on their own will do nothing to foster children's development, either. In fact, this will only force them to live in a state of dependency. An overprotective attitude is harmful to children's self-esteem, and will only confirm to them that they are incapable of doing things by themselves.

Research shows that children who have confident relationships with the adults important to them are more independent, react better to separations and have a higher self-esteem. Children cannot be confident if they do not first feel physically and emotionally secure. Children who are insecure worry about their relationships, and have difficulty learning.

External Security

Everyone (children and adults alike) needs to first feel a sense of external security (i.e. security from outside sources). This gradually evolves into internal security (i.e. security that comes from within) and, over time, develops into confidence in oneself and others. It is this feeling of confidence that allows people to look to the future with hope.

But what are the elements that enable children to have a sense of external security, and how can they be established? First and foremost, the environment in which children are raised (home, daycare centre, school, etc.) must be organized so as to satisfy the need for external security and guarantee the children's physical safety. Parents and teachers must remove all potential sources of danger (medications, toxic products, cooking stove buttons, electric outlets, etc.) and ensure that certain basic safety rules are respected (e.g. sufficient lighting in staircases). Children must also be taught strategies and concrete methods to use when dangerous situations arise and no adults are present – for example, in the case of flood or fire. They must fully understand these security rules.

Parents must ensure that the child can follow a regular schedule, without too many unexpected changes. Children are very conservative and do not cope well with sudden changes or improvisation. With time, consistency and stability help children form a mental sequence of events, enabling them to predict what happens before or after certain activities. This gives them a sense of reassurance and confidence. Adults should tell children as soon as possible about special events that will alter their regular schedules, so that the children have time to deal with and adjust to the expected change psychologically. It is also a good idea to let children know that their schedules will return to normal once an event is over.

All children, especially the younger ones, need to have stable spatial landmarks so they can get used to their surroundings and feel organized and secure. They must be able to create a mental picture of where they live everyday to avoid feeling insecure and panicking when they get lost or when adults are not around. These stable spatial landmarks represent the children's social "niche", a familiar place with which they can identify.

Frequent changes to schedules or surroundings cause stress that even newborns can sense. All children have a great need for stability. Numerous moves, changes in babysitters or daycare centres, unstable shared custody, and changes in routine all create a climate of insecurity that can be potentially harmful to a child's development. Nevertheless, adults must not try to eliminate all forms of change in children's lives. Such a rigid, overprotective attitude would thwart the development of adjustment mechanisms and stress management skills. Without these abilities, children would be powerless when faced with a new situation.

Guaranteeing Stability

All groups and individuals have their own routines and rituals. These are ways of doing things or habits that society and our different activities lead us to adopt. When too many changes are made to children's routines, feelings of instability and insecurity set in and tend to lower their confidence. Routine gives children a sense of security and helps them locate themselves in relation to time and space. Thus, when significant or frequent changes occur, parents must provide the greatest amount of stability possible. For instance, parents whose work schedules fluctuate must ensure that there is always a responsible adult at home.

Children need to form relationships with adults. Today's social context does not seem to respond to this need adequately. Children are in contact with many adults every day. It is estimated that primary school children, who attend daycare facilities at their school, interact with over a dozen adults during the day. But this is misleading, because children do not necessarily derive any particular benefit from such interaction. What is important is not the number of adults with whom children are in contact, but the stability and intensity of the relationship that they have with them.

Today's families suffer from lack of time. Parents are often involved in countless activities, with less and less time to devote to their children. As a result, many children do not have regular, stable relationships with an adult. Without a stable level of attention, the children are at risk of emotional neglect. When children sense that their parents are in a rush or too busy to afford them sufficient time, they can easily conclude that they are not worthy of their parents' time.

An even temperament also helps boost children's sense of security. This does not mean that parents and teachers always have to be even-tempered; however, they should avoid sudden emotional swings in what they say and do, as this will cause children to feel insecure and fearful of excessive, unexpected reactions. Feelings of security and confidence only flourish with fairly predictable behaviour patterns. If parents are too tired, stressed out or in conflict, they must first look after themselves. In other words, they must learn to manage their own stress or ask for help so that they can be calm and open to their children.

Stable guidelines when raising children are extremely important to stimulate feelings of security and confidence. Children who suffer the most from insecurity come from two environments. The first is a very strict, repressive environment, which offers the child little freedom. Measures taken are excessive and humiliating, and children in this type of environment quickly become insecure and inhibited because of fear of the adult reaction. The second environment in which children lack security is when adults are too permissive. Here, children have no guidelines or clear rules of conduct to help them adjust their behaviour and enjoy some freedom within well-defined limits. Children who are brought up in an environment with clear rules develop a healthy self-esteem and see themselves in a positive light.

Stable expectations also help make children feel secure. Adults' expectations regarding desired behaviours should remain approximately the same. Constant changes to expectations or requirements create insecurity in children. Parents should also try not to expect perfection, and learn to ignore certain secondary behaviours when they are not harmful to the child's development. Otherwise, the child might begin to see the quest for perfection as harassment or hostility.

Developing Self-Discipline

Children learn to take control of their physical and human environment from their first few months of life. As they begin to explore, they must be protected from danger and familiarize themselves with the limits of their surroundings. With time, it is essential that they learn to differentiate between accepted and unaccepted. Although not always an easy task, children need to learn to regulate and adapt their behaviour to their surroundings. This self-discipline is acquired gradually from early childhood to adolescence.

It is perfectly normal for children to think mainly about playing and try to manipulate adults to get what they want. It is also normal for children to test their control over their environment and gauge its limits. However, it is less normal for adults to give children a free rein or allow themselves to be manipulated. Such an attitude shows that the adult has some unresolved problems.

Children will not learn to keep their behaviour in check if adults do not first exert control over them, to protect them. This brings a sense of inner security. If children do not feel they are protected, they will expend a lot of energy in the form of disruptive behaviour or hide behind defensive attitudes as a way of safeguarding against danger. Consequently, they will be unable to channel this energy into positive relationships with others and learning.

Reassuring Rules of Conduct

Rules are necessary in all aspects of life. Adults need to set rules of conduct, both at home and at school, in order to provide children with a safe environment. With stable reference points, children can adjust to their environment and also embrace values.

The primary reason for setting disciplinary rules is not to ensure the well-being of adults, but rather to take care of children, protect them and make them feel secure. The rules must be established based on the children's age, needs and level of development, and must have certain characteristics if the children are to acquire a moral and social consciousness, self-discipline and security.

Clear Rules

Rules must be clear, that is, convey values that children can easily understand, such as respect for oneself, others and the environment. It is therefore extremely important that parents and teachers establish the principal values that they wish to communicate to children, eliminating those that they feel are secondary. The adults must agree on the rules, so that the children realize that they live in a stable, coherent environment. If there is no agreement and contradictions arise, children can easily feel insecure.

Concrete Rules

Rules must relate to specific actions that adults wish to see take place. They must reflect expected behaviours and be positive in nature, because everything received by the subconscious is received positively. For instance, if somebody tells a child "Don't run," the child will most likely retain the action word and start running. A concrete rule should emphasize the expected positive behaviour. Instead of saying "Don't run," it would be much better to say "Walk" or "Slow down." Rules must also be realistic: children must be able to obey them.

Consistent Rules

The enforcement of rules should not vary with the adult's mood. Consistency is synonymous with firmness. Parents and teachers often have difficulty maintaining consistency because, like all human beings, they are under substantial stress and their moods change. To encourage consistency, it is important to only have a few rules, because children aged 6 to 12 can only grasp and apply 5 rules at one time. Consistency and firmness are positive when adults do not lose sight of the values they wish to transmit.

Firmness is not synonymous with inflexibility. For example, rules can be temporarily suspended for special events. The children must, however, be made to understand that this is a privilege and that the rules will be reinstated once the event is over. Consistency and firmness provide children with a great sense of security, and enable them to see adults as fair, reliable and trustworthy.

Coherent Rules

It is important for adults to practice what they preach by embracing the same values they wish to transfer to children. Coherence between the values and behaviours advocated inspire security and trust.

Logical Rules

All children have a tendency to break rules, and the consequences of their behaviour affect both themselves and others. Children must learn to accept the results of their actions if they are to internalize a sense of personal responsibility. The consequences of misbehaviour must be logical and natural, that is, they must be closely related to what has occurred.

Let us consider the example of a child who physically or verbally assaults a friend. It might be decided that he must do something for his friend to make up for his behaviour. If a student's behaviour is disruptive to the group to which he belongs, the consequence could be that he must subsequently take on responsibility for something that would benefit the entire group. In an effort to develop children's self-esteem, the logical consequences of misbehaviour must take the form of a positive gesture that will make up for the wrongful act. When the child has corrected his error, the adult must emphasize the child's positive gesture so that the child can rid himself of his negative image as soon as possible.

In Favour of Supportive Discipline

In most cases, disciplinary practices are more authoritative than supportive. Intervention is generally oriented more toward suppressing disruptive or unruly behaviour rather than encouraging positive behaviour. More attention is usually paid to negative behaviour. Once children understand this, many simply repeat their actions in order to satisfy their need for attention.

When an environment is more authoritative than supportive, it creates a climate of mistrust and builds a wall between children and adults. In order to switch from authoritative discipline to supportive discipline, adults need to apply the rules of the three "R's."

Reward

Adults must regularly emphasize children's positive behaviour by means of tangible rewards and congratulate them, so that children become aware of the positive value of their actions. Too many children who are well-behaved and do well at school have low self-esteem because no one has emphasized their positive actions. As mentioned in the previous chapter, self-esteem is the consciousness of self-worth. For children to develop this consciousness, they need to receive positive feedback from adults they trust.

Repair

We encourage positive behaviour when we ask children to repair their mistakes with positive actions. By systematically applying this principle, we are teaching children to act in a positive way with those around them. Making reparation helps children reduce their feelings of guilt as well as assume personal responsibility.

Recover

We often have a tendency to take privileges away from children who misbehave. In developing children's self-esteem, it is important to give children the chance to recover the lost privilege if they behave properly for a predetermined period of time. When we give children an opportunity to make amends, we show them that they can make up for their mistakes and be forgiven. It also teaches them that they are allowed to make mistakes. Recovering privileges brings children to see adults as warm, flexible human beings.

Helping Children Manage Stress

Insecurity and stress are closely linked. Children experience a great deal of stress because of the insecurity they feel when faced with change and new situations. It is therefore important to help them manage such stress and take action on the causes of their insecurity.*

Stress is not strictly negative. It can also help activate our adaptation skills, overcome challenges and progress. Of course, everything depends on how we manage it. Stress becomes distress when we cannot escape or fight it, or when it overwhelms our adaptation skills. When children are in distress, it

---

* See **Suggestions for Helping Children Combat Stress** on page 46.

can trigger motor agitation, behavioural problems, a weakening of the immune system and, in the long run, psychosomatic illnesses.

From Security to Confidence

Protecting and taking care of children makes them feel secure. Parents or teachers who are responsible for this nurturing provide children with a sense of external (outside) security by regularly responding to their expressed needs, providing stability both in relation to time and space, and establishing a number of rules of conduct. Children internalize the external security that comes from warm, stable relationships, and it gradually develops into internal security, or a feeling of confidence.

Feelings of confidence originate, then, with external security, and are consolidated when adults keep their promises. The child then views the adult as reliable and reassuring. If this occurs, the child can internalize the feeling of confidence which alone can give them hope in the future.

The time between a child expressing a need and an adult satisfying this need is important. If the time is too long, frustration can set in and children may give up or no longer believe the need will be met. On the other hand, if the time is too short or their needs are fulfilled immediately, children will not learn how to wait or hope. Knowing the right time to meet the need requires a good understanding of the children's needs and reactions.

To instill feelings of confidence in our children, we must trust them. Both parents and teachers must believe in children's ability to adapt. Adults must learn to support children's initiatives, praise their learning and protect them (without smothering them).

When children are relaxed, optimistic and feel good, it is a sign that confidence has been instilled in them from their elders. Parents and teachers must have confidence in themselves to be able to transfer this feeling to children. They must learn how to manage their own stress and reduce their doubts about how to raise their children if they want to instill feelings of security and confidence in the children. In other words, adults must first learn to take care of themselves so that children can benefit from their example.

Suggestions for Helping Children Combat Stress

- Noise is one of the main causes of stress. The main sources must be identified and eliminated.

- Cramped spaces can cause aggressive interaction between children, making many of them feel insecure. All children must have enough space to move around freely and, ideally, a personal space where they can take refuge when the tension gets too high.

- It is important to limit children's stress during periods of change. Generally speaking, changes occurring within a 6-month time frame should be reduced to the bare minimum, especially with young children. For example, in the event of a separation, parents should avoid moving children to different houses, daycare centres or schools. They should not take the children away from their friends or their school-related activities in which they normally participate.

- Too many children experience performance anxiety. Their schedules are often too hectic and they feel compelled to succeed for the adults in their lives. Parents need to learn to respect their children's pace of learning.

- Adults need to teach children to ask for help and express their fears and anger.

- Children must be allowed free time to use their imagination and play so they can relax.

- Physical exercise is an excellent way for children to manage stress. Relaxation, music and mental imaging exercises can also help them relax.

- Laughing - like running, singing or reading - is a real stress-reliever.

- Adults must help children channel their energy in a positive manner — i.e. leave aside what they cannot change and, using their adaptation skills, strive with things they can change.

- All parents have generally found ways to combat stress. It is up to them to teach their children how to do the same.

- Since stress is contagious, parents and teachers must make sure they reduce their own stress levels.

Signs That Children Feel Confident

Children who have a strong feeling of confidence experience most of the following attitudes and behaviours:

- Demonstrate confidence in front of adults they know
- Relax physically
- Allow physical contact
- Adjust to stress
- Remain calm when they experience a physical injury
- Remain calm when faced with physical discomfort
- Tolerate delays
- Anticipate pleasure
- React positively to new things
- Take calculated risks
- Form a mental picture of time
- Are optimistic about the future
- Understand and accept the meaning of rules
- Respond positively to rules

Parental Attitudes That Encourage Confidence

- Guarantee children's stability by maintaining a regular schedule
- Provide children with a stable living environment in relation to time and space
- Establish fixed routines and rituals
- Remain stable and reliable in response to children's physical needs
- Remain stable and reliable in response to children's emotional needs
- Ensure a sense of physical security in children by eliminating sources of danger
- Set aside time to play with children
- Provide security and affection when children are sick or hurt
- Keep promises
- Gauge the appropriate time between children expressing their desires and meeting them
- Avoid excessive mood swings
- Establish reassuring rules of conduct
- Be consistent when enforcing rules of conduct
- Impose logical and natural punishments for misbehaviour
- Reduce children's stress as much as possible by preparing them for change
- Provide children with ways of reducing stress by having them engage in relaxing activities

FOSTERING SELF-KNOWLEDGE

▼

During the first few years of life, children gradually learn to distance and differentiate themselves from the people who are important to them. This process of separation-individualization helps children better understand themselves and construct a self-concept, which will serve as the basis for their identity. They come to view themselves as unique beings and develop the basic elements of self-knowledge (a self-concept) that will later evolve into a sense of identity that will be realized during adolescence.

The Self-Concept

Because of the learning process taking place as children try new things, and because of the feedback they receive from the people around them, children gradually get to know their environment and themselves. Their accumulated experiences help them define their physical characteristics, needs and feelings, as well as their physical, intellectual and social skills. All of these elements combine to make up the self-concept which, according to the *Dictionnaire actuel de l'éducation*, is the set of ideas and beliefs that one has of oneself, as well as the resulting attitudes.*

---

* Legendre, op.cit.

Self-knowledge, or the self-concept, gradually evolves into a sense of identity which serves as a basis for the development of self-esteem. To develop a healthy sense of identity, children must have a realistic understanding of their abilities, problems and limitations, and be aware of how they are perceived by others. This understanding — the more realistic the better — is only possible when children harbour positive feelings toward themselves.

Children must learn to *know* themselves (self-concept and sense of identity) before they are able to acknowledge themselves. Self-knowledge helps children internalize a sense of self-worth (self-esteem).

Children's self-knowledge develops as a result of their inter-action with others. It is strongly influenced by the people they are close to and consider to be important. It is in the presence of these people that children participate in a multitude of physical, social and intellectual activities during which they develop various skills of which they gradually become aware.

Self-knowledge and the resulting sense of personal identity are the foundations of self-esteem. This is what makes children feel unique and able to earn the respect of others. It is by seeing themselves as different from others that children gradually discover their unique character.

Noticing Our Differences — the Path to Self-Knowledge

All children possess distinctive characteristics when they are born. They all have their own character traits, express their needs differently, and develop at their own pace. Through their actions, reactions, needs and feelings, children show that they are different both from their parents and other children.

It is by noticing that they are different from other people that children become aware of who they are and develop a sense of personal identity. In fact, if we felt like someone else in every respect, we would not be able to perceive our own identity. Children must know what distinguishes them from other people. They have to realize they do not have the same physical or morphological features as others; they have a set of physical, intellectual and social skills that are entirely their own, and they have clearly distinct personalities. These differences, realized over time, help children see themselves as unique human beings.

In their quest for identity, children may also realize that their peers possess the same skills as they do, and that some of their own reactions or personality traits are shared by their friends. This balanced perception of differences and similarities when they compare themselves with others eventually gives children a sound self-knowledge.

Children need to be valued for who they are, with their evolving identities and, above all, their differences. Acceptance of their differences gives them the right to exist as unique individuals. This is not an easy task; the history of humanity is full of examples showing the difficulties that various societies have had in tolerating individual and collective differences.

Differences between individuals create the distance necessary to put an end to merging or symbiotic relationships. If we do not accept other people's differences, we reject our own identity and our right to exist as unique individuals.

When faced with differences, human beings adopt four distinct attitudes, ranging from the most primitive to the most progressive. First of all, we can reject that which is different in the other person because it seems threatening or does not conform to our customs or values. This is a total rejection of the other person and has nothing to do with the justifiable rejection of unacceptable behaviour. A second attitude consists in tolerating the other person's differences. This attitude is a little more progressive, but still suggests that we do not completely accept the other person, but rather view their differences as a necessary evil. A third, still more progressive attitude involves accepting the other person's differences. It indicates the acceptance of our own differences and the ability to embrace the differences of others. It also requires empathy and respect for the other person, who is perceived as having the right to be different and unique. Finally, the most progressive attitude consists in valuing the other person with or in spite of their differences.

To value another person, we have to have a meaningful relationship with them; a close, affectionate bond that confirms each individual's value. Valuing the other person means appreciating the essence of their being, as well as their appearance and conduct (how they seem to be). This presupposes that our judgements about this individual's personality and behaviour are positive and guided by the close, loving relationship we have with them. We may not always like their behaviour or their attitudes, but the love and respect we feel for them transcend any differences that might divide us.

From Dream Child to Real Child

Parents create a mental image of their child before that child is born. That image is a compilation of their dreams, wishes and expectations. For example, their child will be beautiful, happy, intelligent and sociable. This image of the unborn child is what we call the "dream child" and is perfectly natural and understandable. But how is this image created?

The dream child is often the kind of child that we would have liked to be. We subconsciously expect the child to achieve our dreams, to make up for our shortcomings and, sometimes, to be our own narcissistic continuation. It is perfectly normal to have expectations for our unborn children, but they should be realistic. Life is full of both pleasant surprises and disappointments that we cannot always predict. While our dream child lives in our imagination, our real children exist in the real world. They bring us joy and cause us sorrow. Parents whose expectations are too high run the risk of being disappointed and of focusing their attention on the negative aspects or flaws of their real children.

Adults, both parents and teachers, expect a great deal from children. Why do we attach so much importance to our children's achievements, to their performance, and why do we scrutinize their development? Is it because we hope, somehow, to be able to live our lives over again, through our children, this time succeeding where we have failed? This is a harmful attitude because, although our children may be like us, they are also different.

Children want, more than anything, to be loved, and they are willing to do almost anything for that love, even deny their innermost nature. Children who are never happy with who they are, who are critical of themselves, tear up their drawings and panic if they do not get the highest marks in school are convinced that they can only be loved if they are perfect. They think that they always fall short of what is expected of them, and they can easily develop symptoms associated with performance anxiety (nausea, stomach pain, insomnia, etc.) and feelings of depression, even if their parents do not express their expectations overtly.

Too many parents and teachers who are uncompromising perfectionists toward themselves and their children have a tendency to focus on problems and imperfections and ignore capabilities and skills. When we raise our children, we should distance ourselves from our perfectionism and forget about the dream child in order to focus on our real children. It is important to have expectations for our children, but those expectations should be in keeping with their interests and abilities and be suited to their particular pace of development.

Parents have a tendency not to take the time to see their children *as they are*, but rather to dwell on *what they do*. We need to pay attention to our children and notice their strengths in all areas: physical (strength, flexibility, endurance, etc.), intellectual (curiosity, good judgement, memory, ability to reason, etc.), social (ease at making friends, ability to share, to assert themselves, etc.), and personal (generosity, organization, imagination, etc.). Parents often focus only on one or two aspects that they personally value, without taking into account whether or not those aspects best describe their children.

Both parents and educators should also take into account the difficulties that children face. From the standpoint of the development of self-esteem, we should not view difficulties as limitations or disabilities. All problems should be seen as temporary, and treated as challenges. Parents and teachers should help children overcome their difficulties; they should make them understand that they have the ability to succeed if they go about it the right way and persevere in their efforts. This shows children that adults have confidence in their abilities, thus encouraging them and giving them hope. If neither their parents nor their teachers have any expectations of them, children will interpret this as proof that they are incapable of overcoming challenges or improving.

Giving Priority to Children

In trying to understand and master their physical and human environment, children gradually become more independent through numerous interrelated and progressively more difficult learning experiences. Naturally, some of the attempts are successful, while others may not have the expected result.

Developing self-esteem means letting children actualize the best aspects of themselves. To help children achieve this, parents and teachers should give children positive feedback whenever they succeed at something, however minor it may be. This is how children become aware of their skills; positive feedback reinforces their belief in their own worth and makes it easier for them to face new challenges. When it comes to self-knowledge, children's actual performance does not matter as much as the way they perceive the reactions of the adults who are important to them. Positive reactions are remembered, and give children a permanent sense of self-worth. It is because of this regular feedback that children, around the age of 7 or 8, can internalize positive messages, have a sense of self-worth and be able to continue to nurture their self-esteem through their own inner conversations.

Children are not defined solely by what they do. Adults should also value them for who they are. However, our society seems to be obsessed with performance and achievement, and too many children who are not able to meet these expectations feel devalued. These same children often possess a great emotional intelligence, demonstrated by their generosity and their sensitivity to the needs of others. But these qualities are often far from being valued for their true worth. It is therefore crucial that all children feel loved and appreciated for who they are as much as for what they do.

Cultivating Empathy

Infants express their needs by gestures and facial expressions. A 3-year-old who wants attention, on the other hand, may decide to run around the kitchen table simply to attract that attention. The need is real, but the way of expressing it is inadequate. In other words, children express their needs in different ways and with varying degrees of skill, depending on their stage of development. It is therefore important that parents and teachers reveal the feelings and needs behind children's behaviour. This will enable them to improve their own ability to empathize.

Empathy is a way of intuitively knowing other people based on an attitude of understanding, respect and acceptance. Thanks to their intuition and ability to empathize as well as their profound knowledge of their children — even their body language — parents are able to decode their children's feelings and needs and to explain them to their children. (For example, "It makes you angry when you don't succeed right away" or "You get nervous when you have to deal with something new.") Children then feel understood, become aware of their needs and feelings, and learn to express them better.

Parents should trust their intuition and help their children become aware of the reasons behind their behaviour, even though this may be difficult. It can be done simply by talking or with the help of drawings or symbolic games. Gradually, children will learn to make the connection between their needs, feelings and behaviours. The more conscious children are of their feelings and needs, the less trouble they will have expressing them in an appropriate manner.

Things That are Harmful to Self-Esteem

Neglect

Children whose parents are not involved in their lives or whose parents have neither wishes nor expectations for them, live in an emotional desert. Too many children suffer from the unavailability of parents who are preoccupied with countless other activities and who, consequently, do not have enough time to devote to their children. Children in this situation tell themselves that making an effort is pointless, because no one will bother to pay attention to them anyway. All children must be absolutely certain that they matter to someone.

A "Negative" Upbringing

The upbringing of most of today's adults was characterized by a search for flaws and shortcomings. It was largely conditioned by negative messages that often prevented parents from looking on the bright side and emphasizing their children's good points. As a result, today's parents have certain firmly rooted reactions that often result in remarks such as, "He's a year old and he still can't walk," "He's been learning it for months, but he still doesn't know the alphabet," "He's always in a bad mood," "He never cleans up his room." Words like "always" and "never" make children powerless and prevent them from changing.

Words that Hurt

The word "violence" is related to the word "violation." Verbal violence is a violation of a person's pride and dignity and is very harmful to self-esteem. Just as there are words that are caring, there are others that can hurt deeply. It is extremely important to talk to children with respect; if we want them to learn to respect themselves, they must feel that they are respected by other people. Nicknames with negative connotations, even if used jokingly, have the effect of negatively influencing children's inner conversation, making them feel that they are worth less than other people. Frequent negative criticism, hurtful remarks and strong opinions can deal severe blows to children.

It is important to point out that the majority of adults who speak to children in a hurtful way were themselves victims of this type of language as children. But this behaviour, passed on from generation to generation, must be stopped, not only because it undermines self-esteem but also because there is a fine line between verbal violence and physical violence.

Negative Identity

As a general rule, children's behaviour is a reflection of the way they see themselves. In their quest for self-knowledge, they adopt a variety of attitudes and experiment with countless different behaviours, while observing adults' reactions. It is on the basis of that feedback that children adopt the behaviours that are espoused by people close to them and reject those that are not. But it all depends on the type of attention that is paid to children by the people they consider important. If children discover that the most effective way of attracting attention is to behave inappropriately, they will tend to misbehave.

Everyone, with the exception of people with serious psychopathological disorders (autism, psychosis, etc.), builds a personal identity which is either positive or negative. When children constantly receive negative feedback, they internalize a negative image of themselves and incorporate it into their identity. They adopt attitudes and behaviours that conform to their sense of identity. If they have internalized a negative identity, they will have a compulsive tendency to defend and confirm that identity by repeated negative behaviour.

Let us take the example of hyperactivity which, in and of itself, does not jeopardize a child's future. But if hyperactive children receive a great deal of negative feedback, they will develop a negative identity. Children who are repeatedly told to quiet down, stop fidgeting and stay still will start to believe that they are "bad." And since they believe that deep down inside they are bad, they will behave badly to confirm their self-image. Another useful example might be that of children who often have trouble adjusting and who have internalized a negative image of themselves. If you tell them that they did something well and that you are proud of them, they may become disruptive. This is because they are incapable of holding on to the memory of being good and will, subconsciously, destroy that memory in order to protect their identity, even if it is negative. A human being cannot survive without an identity; when you lose that, you no longer feel you really exist.

By developing their self-esteem, we can help disruptive children gradually internalize and retain a positive self-image. This requires devising strategies that will prevent them from systematically destroying positive feedback. For example, at bedtime, you can remind them of three positive behaviours that they exhibited during the day, and then quickly leave the room to prevent them from cancelling out your positive feedback. In this way, the last messages that children receive during the day are positive. In time, these messages will fill their mind and their subconscious, and they will succeed in becoming less disruptive. When children get older, adults can explain to them why they exhibit negative behaviours when they are congratulated. This type of explanation, relying on the adult's ability to empathize, should not contain any negative judgements. It can help children become aware of the existence of a connection between their feelings and their negative behaviours, and make them decide to change.

Parents, teachers and educators should be sensitive to the dynamic of a negative identity in children. They will often witness the bitter inner struggle between the "good child" and the "bad child", and they should know that the "good child" is always there, despite any disruptive behaviour.

Signs of Good Self-Knowledge

We should not expect young children to develop profound self-knowledge or a complete sense of personal identity. After all, it takes most of us a lifetime to achieve that much! But children can, from time to time and with varying degrees of success, express the majority of the following attitudes and behaviours:

- Recognize in themselves a physical skill or lack thereof
- Recognize in themselves an intellectual skill or lack thereof
- Recognize in themselves a relationship skill or lack thereof
- Recognize in themselves a creative skill or lack thereof
- Determine what makes them different from others
- Assert themselves
- Determine the reasons why other people love them
- Make choices
- Explain their preferences and ideas
- Express their feelings
- Express their needs
- Be increasingly aware of the connection between their needs, feelings and behaviours
- Command respect
- Take on age-appropriate responsibilities
- Remember their own past successes

Parental Attitudes That Encourage Self-Knowledge in Children

Parents should adopt attitudes and approaches that encourage self-knowledge in their children. They should try to:

- Build a close and loving relationship with their children
- Recognize and accept the differences between their own children and other children
- Forget about the dream child
- Set realistic learning and behavioural goals
- Demonstrate that they are warm and empathetic
- Speak to their children in a respectful way
- Focus on their children's good points, skills and abilities
- Give positive feedback regularly
- Help their children realize that they are unique because of their physical characteristics and special skills
- Encourage assertiveness and independence
- Help their children become aware of their needs and feelings and express them appropriately
- Help their children realize that there is a connection between their needs, feelings and behaviours
- Pay attention to any difficulties their children may encounter and help them overcome them
- Blame the unacceptable behaviour, not the child.

It would be unrealistic to expect parents to adopt all of these attitudes and consistently use every single one of these approaches. Nevertheless, it is important for them to regularly examine the quality of their relationship with their children. Children's self-esteem is profoundly influenced by the atmosphere in which they live.

CHAPTER 4

Fostering a Sense of Belonging

▼

People, by their very nature, are social beings. They need to belong to a group, feel connected to each other, and be part of a social network. Children are no exception, and their need to be part of a group grows stronger as they get older.

Parents have more influence on their preschool children than do their children's friends. Later, when their children are aged 6 to 10, the parents' influence is roughly the same as that of friends. During adolescence, the parents' influence wanes in importance. As children's socialization progresses, their parents' influence on them declines, but the legacy of parental influence will always remain.

Developing Prosocial Attitudes

During the first few years of life, children's relationship with their parents is very close. This strong intimate bond is a sort of primitive core of children's self-esteem. As they get older and venture into the world beyond their family circle, they try to establish other relationships and acquire, especially with their friends, their first awareness of their own self-worth. It is impossible for them to experience a sense of belonging without the development of socialization. The pace of socialization is different for each child, but there are always times of sudden progress, periods of stagnation and, sometimes, even temporary regression.

From the age of 2, children love being in the company of other children their age, even if they still cannot play. They love to be together. Around age 4, children will be very vocal about wanting to be with their friends. Even the most patient and available parent will not make as wonderful a friend as another child. Activities such as pulling each other's hair, fighting over toys, learning to negotiate and share contribute greatly to children's inner well-being.

To feel as if they really belong, children must go through a long process of learning various skills, such as cooperation. Preschool children have not yet done this and cannot quickly and completely master the kind of social skills that make it easier to belong to a group. In fact, they do not possess qualities such as altruism and the ability to cooperate. They are still much too self-centered and can only engage in activities of "co-operation" and in what are known as "collective monologues" because they take place in the presence of other people but without taking them into account.

To be capable of real cooperation or true dialogue, children must first develop a conceptual framework of reciprocity. Then, and only then, will their self-centeredness collapse, making it possible for them to consider the needs, opinions and feelings of others, while tying them to their own. Although preschool children have not yet acquired this ability, we should encourage them in that direction. First, we should take advantage of their tendency to play on a one-on-one basis with other children to help them develop prosocial attitudes. Then, we can encourage that tendency by helping them form a larger friendship pool.

Breaking Down Egocentricity

Children under 7 or 8 do not understand that other people can have points of view that are different from their own. They are very focused on their own immediate needs, and their opinions have the force of law. This kind of attitude prevents them from being able to really cooperate with others. The main characteristics of egocentricity at that age are:

- Focusing on their own point of view or on their immediate perceptions.

- Having trouble seeing and taking into account the needs and perspectives of others.

- Blaming their own mistakes on other people or on circumstances.

- Thinking in an inflexible way, that is, having trouble modifying their opinions and questioning their decisions.

- Being unaware of their own contradictions.

- Having a tendency to pass judgement while taking into account only one aspect of the issue.

- Readily making generalizations based on a single factor or perception.

- Demonstrating stereotypical social behaviours.

- Limiting themselves to a single strategy when faced with a problem.

- Doing very little self-evaluation and, consequently, having difficulty changing their actions and reactions.

If we consider the fact that many seemingly mature adults are quite obviously self-centered, we can appreciate how difficult it is to get rid of this attitude.

When children acquire the ability to think reciprocally, which comes with the onset of logical thought, they begin to notice and consider other people's points of view. To belong to a group, they have to learn to take into account the needs and opinions of the other group members and to take on responsibilities within that group. To help them get rid of their egotistical tendencies, cooperate and feel a sense of belonging to a group, we have to teach them to be sensitive to others. When children have successfully learned to recognize their own needs and feelings, we should help them also notice the needs and feelings that other people express through their words, actions and body language.

One of the things that adults should try to do is encourage children to take other people into account, and congratulate them when they show themselves capable of cooperating and listening. It is also important to help them understand and recognize situations in which they should act as members of a group. This sensitivity to others — this social conscience — can be realized by passing on values such as generosity and the importance of helping other people. Thus, parents should regularly encourage their children to stop focusing on their immediate needs in order to share with or help their friends.

Group Activities

The feeling of belonging to a group does not magically appear by itself. Children can only experience it if they have a chance to take part in group activities. A group is more than just a collection of individuals; it is defined by the quality and frequency of contact between its members in pursuit of common goals. Group activities that allow each child to contribute in their own way are crucial to development.

Children's peer groups are an important source of positive feedback and improve their self-esteem. The active participation of each child and their respect for the rules are essential to membership in a group. Children learn to help one another by constructively working together on group projects. Adults have a key role in this; they should urge their children to encourage their friends, congratulate them and help them when they need it.

Children develop a feeling of belonging when they feel valued by others — when they are made to believe that they are unique and able to significantly contribute to the group as a whole. The awareness of being part of a group develops when children take on responsibilities for the benefit of all group members. These responsibilities should be suited to the child's abilities and assumed by each child in turn, so that everyone contributes to the group's well-being.

The Family Group

The first time children experience a sense of belonging is within their own family, their first social niche. It is the family that first teaches children to live in a community; thus, close ties between family members as well as good family cohesiveness are very important. It is with the help and support of their family members that children can succeed in overcoming their egocentricity and start taking other people into account. This is how they learn to communicate, assert themselves, take on responsibilities, respect established rules and share.

The relationships that children have with their siblings provide an opportunity for them to resolve conflicts caused by rivalry and competition. The sibling relationship is the first group within which children learn to bargain, negotiate and deal with antagonism. In today's society, almost 50% of children have no brothers or sisters. While these children cannot know either the joys or the frustrations of a sibling relationship, most of them belong to some sort of group, whether it be in a daycare centre or at school.

The family, the first core group to which children belong, significantly influences their future ability to adapt. Because of loving family ties, children identify first with values fostered in their family environment. When values embraced by their family differ from those they come in contact with at school, children will tend to support the values that they learned at home.

The sense of belonging to their family increases when children are told about the history and traditions of their extended family (grandparents, uncles, aunts, cousins, etc.). Every family has its own particular values, traditions, special events and anecdotes. Children who know their own family's history feel a sense of continuity and realize that they have roots.

A feeling of belonging cannot be created without group activities. This applies to family life as well. It is, therefore, very important that families organize group activities or projects that require a contribution from each family member. This can markedly reduce the sense of loneliness that children sometimes feel.

The School Group

When children reach school age, their same-sex group of friends acquires a new meaning. Despite attempts made to get rid of stereotypes and gender discrimination, boys still play boys' games, and girls, girls' games. In fact, children feel the need to clearly define their social identity, which is done mainly through comparison and the acting out of clearly defined gender roles.

Once at school, children want to expand their circle of friends and be accepted by some sort of group. Boys are particularly sensitive to the approval of other boys, while girls benefit more from the positive feedback of other girls. If children do not feel accepted by a group, they will hesitate to express their opinions, show initiative or actively participate in group projects. They will be afraid of being rejected or of appearing ridiculous.

Later on, during adolescence, groups become mixed. Because membership in a group makes it possible for them to distance themselves from their parents and to find their own identity, teenagers feel an urgent need to belong to a group.

Children and adolescents with social problems, who do not know how to make or keep friends, develop a poor self-image of their social skills and greatly disparage themselves. Studies have shown that children in grade one who have trouble making friends and are isolated run the risk of experiencing social problems as adults. It is therefore important to help school-aged children develop social skills and a sense of belonging.

Both children and adults need to feel that they are an integral part of a group. School, far from being solely a teaching institution, should be a good place for children to grow up in.

Do you remember your years at elementary school? If you do, chances are that you mostly remember the social activities that you took part in and the friends you made. Adults who are asked this question often say that they remember such and such a friend, or important events such as school plays. Hardly anyone remembers the specific content of the school curriculum. It is the good times, the ones that were filled with warm human contact, that we tend to remember, rather than the things that were taught in a classroom.

The feeling of belonging to a school is fundamental and helps prevent students from dropping out. One has only to think of the reaction of young people when they are told that their family will be moving; they will protest vigorously because they do not want to change schools nor lose touch with their friends. Children are often more conservative and more attached to their social environment than adults, and teenagers even more so than children.

School is a very important tool for furthering the process of socialization in children and fostering a sense of belonging to a particular place. This aspect of school is just as important as its mission of imparting knowledge.

Every school should reflect the values, customs and standards of the community which it serves, all the while pursuing its mission of teaching. The objectives of each school are developed around the values shared by parents and school staff. In this way, the school remains in harmony with the community it serves, in the same way as other organizations and institutions. It is in these conditions that both children and parents can feel at home.

Some schools find it easy to create an atmosphere where both children and parents can feel comfortable. For proof, one need only look to the vehement protests of parents and the general population of a neighbourhood or a town in response to talk of closing "their" school. They react as if something crucial to their social network were being taken away.

What are the tangible signs of children's sense of belonging to their school? First of all, children who are attached to their school feel good and relaxed when they are there. They want to go to school, mostly to see their friends and be around adults who work there, and whom they like. They feel that they are part of a group which draws its value from the quality and frequency of friendly interactions that happen at school, rather than its size.

Students also take pride in their school. They often talk about it and praise it. Those who would dare denigrate their school, beware! Moreover, they feel responsible and useful there. They believe that their attitudes play an important role in their group and that their personal contribution is significant. This feeling boosts their self-esteem.

They stand behind their friends and would be ready to support them if the group were ever in any difficulties. They actively participate in activities, projects and decisions of their group of friends and this increases their sense of self-worth. Finally, they generally respect the equipment and supplies that their group uses at school.

Some schools have been able to create a strong sense of belonging in both students and parents. Parents feel that school staff have their and their children's well-being at heart, and that the staff are as concerned with the parents as with the school board administrators.

Finally, let us not forget that creating a sense of belonging in a school also involves the acceptance of differences, such as the ethnic diversity of many children and parents. The school should be open to this diversity and the richness of the human experience.

The Group of Friends

Today, children spend a great deal of time in organized groups (daycare, school, after-school activities, etc.) that have a profound influence on their development. These groups are therefore, important and necessary because they offer children a chance to become aware of and adapt to a different environment than that of their family and, in so doing, prepare them for life in society.

Logical thought, which first appears around the age of 7 or 8, helps break down much of the egocentricity of childhood. From then on, children have access to the reciprocity of viewpoints, which is the basis for empathy. Because they are no longer solely focusing on satisfying their own wants, they can take into account the feelings, opinions and viewpoints of other people. Thanks to this new-found ability, true cooperation becomes possible. Children can establish more stable and selective relationships within their group and at the same time develop a sense of belonging to their small community. They are able to understand the logical and causal connections between their own actions and the consequences to the group as a whole. It becomes possible for them to modify their contribution to the group according to the collective goal. Their social conscience gradually develops.

Children need to interact with their peers. As far as emotions are concerned, they need their friends to serve as role models. They can learn many new behaviours by observing and imitating others. They compare themselves constantly to their peers in order to evaluate their own abilities, strengths and limitations and, in so doing, become aware of the things that they are good at — one of the foundations of good self-esteem.

During this time, children develop a sense of belonging to a group through shared activities. To the values they were taught at home they add those that are upheld by their group. They worry about being accepted by others as individuals who can make a valuable personal contribution. They respect the group's rules and try not to be rejected by their friends. It is the values, rules, chosen activities and a feeling of being accepted and appreciated that contribute to children's sense of belonging to their group. And it is this feeling which explains, in part, the unwillingness of children or teenagers to move away from their neighbourhood or change schools. The group of friends becomes a sort of social haven where they can feel safe and where their sense of self-worth can be bolstered. When a group is particularly tight-knit, it can go as far as rejecting those of its peers who do not follow its rules or take part in its activities.

Children or teenagers are assigned roles, usually on the initiative of their leader. Preparations for a group game or activity are governed by ritual. The rules adopted by the group have the force of law. Anyone who does not respect those rules or who cheats may be rejected by the group. Only the results count, and competition is fierce. The efforts of each participant are promoted a lot less than the positive results which benefit the group as a whole.

Between the ages of 6 and 10, gender segregation takes place. Boys and girls have a tendency to form friendships with members of their own sex. Studies in this field show that groups composed of girls, generally less hierarchical and less organized than groups composed of boys, display less solidarity and cohesiveness. On the other hand, girls tend to place more value than boys on relationship skills and the ability to communicate and empathize. Boys attach a great deal more importance to technical and competitive skills.

Children's self-image, or the confidence they have in their social skills, greatly influences their membership in a group. Conversely, the group's view of them strongly affects their social behaviour.

We cannot expect children to be independent in every activity. In the same way, leaders cannot take a leadership role in every group they belong to or in every activity they participate in. In general, leaders have charisma, and group members try to imitate them. Leaders often initiate and organize spontaneous activities, and they earn the group's respect by demonstrating great ability in such activities.

However, we should not confuse leaders with bullies, who are despotic and try to dominate the group by using threats to satisfy their own ambitions. Bullies are feared, but not liked. They may even be expelled from a group, if it is particularly close-knit.

Children who are rejected generally do not know how to fit in. By and large, they would like to strike up friendships with their peers, but they are often clumsy in the way they relate to others, or simply do not possess skills that are valued by the group.

There are other typical roles that children take on within the group setting. These are determined by the personality of each child, and relate to group dynamics and, especially, to the group's particular activities. A child can, for example, play the role of clown in one group or activity, but not in another context. When children consistently play the same role (bully, scapegoat, clown, rejected child, etc.) and this prevents them from developing or making friends, it is important to see a specialist in order to help them rebuild their self-esteem and assert themselves.

Belonging to a group can be a very powerful learning experience. The group further develops and perfects social skills that parents have passed on to their children. It has been noticed that peers often have a greater influence on children's learning than adults, and that school, as a general rule, has become one of the places that has the greatest influence on the socialization of children. It is there that children learn to fit in with a group. They gradually become more skilled at making friends and handling interpersonal conflict. They learn to adapt to rules, to win and to lose, to talk and to assert themselves, and to take on responsibilities within the group.

Through their contacts with other people, children learn to understand and accept differences related to such issues as skin colour, language, faults and abilities. They also learn, mostly through their experiences within the group, to socialize their impulses and use their particular abilities for the good of the community.

The Influence of Parents and Teachers

The attitude of parents and teachers has a direct influence on the process of children's socialization. By observing them, children learn to open up to others, accept differences, be tolerant and confident and to resolve most of the conflicts within the group on their own. All this makes them eager to be sociable and to assert themselves in a positive way. When children take the wrong approach to fitting in with a group, acting out violently or withdrawing into themselves for instance, adults need to help them adopt attitudes that are in keeping with the values of democracy, negotiation and sharing.

When we overprotect children, we are sending them the following message, "I think that you're incapable of facing the music and that you're too weak. That's why I have to do it for you." Children come to expect that their problems will be solved for them, and start to believe that they cannot become part of a group on their own.

It is harmful to always make excuses for children. If we do, we are not helping them see themselves realistically, question their own behaviour or actively seek effective social strategies.

Adults who themselves have trouble trusting other people, enjoying themselves in a group setting or keeping friends will have a difficult time helping their children build a social life. Children learn by imitating and identifying with people who are important to them. Yet another opportunity for adults to improve themselves!

Teaching children to be generous helps them become part of society and develop a good self-image. Acting unselfishly and compassionately helps us feel "good" inside. When we accustom children to helping others, we make them aware of human relations and make it possible for them to enjoy the spirit of giving.

Socialization and Belonging

Everyone has a fundamental need to socialize, to feel that they belong to a group, and to have companionship as well as friendship. Doing things together, laughing, singing, sharing — all this makes us feel happy and complete. In times of trouble, our friends are on our side and protect us from loneliness. Being loved and appreciated helps us face many difficult situations. What other people tell us, the way they look at us and listen to us, and the respect they have for us helps us define who we are and makes us want to improve ourselves. The feeling of belonging is an antidote to social isolation.

In today's world, new technologies have greatly increased and facilitated communication. And yet, despite the myriad means of communication available, people — both children and adults — are lonelier than ever before. This paradox can be explained by the fact that modern society encourages us to make contact with others instead of building meaningful relationships with them.

Meaningful relationships transcend time and space. If we have a solid friendship with someone, we always carry a memory of that person with us. As long as that memory of them is alive within us, we will maintain our meaningful relationship with them. Stable and long-lasting friendships make up a sort of relationship network that we can always be connected to and that sustains our feeling of belonging to a group.

Social self-esteem, or the self-worth that we draw from social interaction, is developed through socialization and perfected through membership in a group. Am I important in the eyes of others? Are others important in my eyes? How much do I value myself with respect to my family, friends and my colleagues at work? All these questions are related to social self-esteem. People who believe that their presence in a group is of no importance or changes nothing in the group believe, in fact, that they themselves are of little value to others. They are probably lonely. They certainly need to improve their social self-esteem and experience a feeling of belonging.

Signs That Children Feel a Sense of Belonging

Children who feel that they belong to a group exhibit most of the following attitudes and behaviours:

- Actively seek out the presence of other people
- Remain relaxed when they are with the group
- Find it easy to communicate with other people
- Easily remember group cheers, songs, etc.
- Are capable of social sensitivity
- Are capable of generosity
- Are capable of sharing and helping other people
- Sometimes suggest ideas that could be useful to the group
- Take on minor responsibilities within the group
- Talk about their friends or about the group at home
- Are capable of applying strategies for resolving social problems.

Parental Attitudes That Encourage a Sense of Belonging in Children

Conflicts inevitably arise in every group, especially if that group is made up of children who are still totally self-centered. It is, therefore, essential to advise children on ways to resolve their relationship problems and encourage them to practice using these strategies. The process should be similar to the following:

- Work with your children to try to find various solutions by helping them become aware of all the means and resources available to them

- Help them choose the solution that is most effective and suits everybody

- Apply the chosen solution and help them implement it

- Evaluate the effectiveness of the chosen solution afterwards.

Parents can adopt many attitudes to help their children realize that they are worth something in the eyes of others and that their family or group is important to them.

Chapter 5

Fostering a Sense of Competency

▼

Every time children learn something new, they break a tie of dependency. They become open to a multitude of possibilities and learn to be independent. Learning is a gradual, active process of acquisition during which children convert knowledge into skills and abilities that they will use for the rest of their lives.

There is no point in telling children that they have skills and are able to accomplish tasks if they are not given the opportunity to succeed in their activities. It is also useless to make children do things if their efforts are uniformly unsuccessful.

Developing a sense of competency does not happen by magic. Instead, it comes from participating in stimulating, suitably adjusted activities that challenge and motivate children and encourage independence.

Children cannot develop new motor, intellectual or social skills if they do not succeed when trying new things. To succeed, children must feel their self-worth, be conscious of their abilities, and consequently have a healthy self-esteem. This positive opinion that we have of ourselves is the basis of motivation and learning, and can be represented in the following manner:

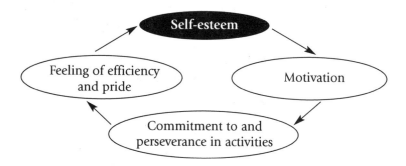

Self-esteem comes from past experience. Remembering successes and proving competency in certain areas enables us to have faith in ourselves (self-esteem) and hopes for success in pursuing goals. Anticipating success forms the foundation of motivation.

Motivation is demonstrated by a commitment to and perseverance in a chosen activity. Good learning methods and strategies lead to success, triggering a feeling of efficiency and pride which, in turn, increases the feeling of self-esteem. This is the cyclical pattern of learning in which self-esteem plays a central role.

Children must experience numerous successes to prevent motivation and learning problems from arising. This is why parents and teachers must be directly involved in the various elements that constitute learning and, most importantly, encourage motivation.

Motivation

Motivation — what encourages a person to accomplish a task or to reach an objective corresponding to a need — is created from desire and determination. In other words, motivation is a set of forces that prompts a person to act.

It could also be said that motivation is the anticipation of pleasure or of the usefulness of a task to be completed. For example, it is difficult to be motivated to play chess if this game does not appeal to us. The same is true of tasks to be accomplished. For instance, if tidying one's office is not necessary for work or personal well-being, the motivation is not there.

Developing the ability to anticipate is a gradual process. Its roots lie in infancy, when children must wait for their wants to be satisfied. Children must also be given the chance to anticipate. If their smallest desires are fulfilled immediately, they do not have an opportunity to form a mental picture of what they want and anticipate the resulting gratification. On the other hand, by having to wait for something and by experiencing the accompanying frustration, children gradually learn that waiting is generally followed by satisfaction. Children can allow themselves to hope, that is, to be motivated. Adults must therefore keep their promises. For example, if an adult promises to take a child to the movies, the adult must keep that promise. By keeping promises made after a "reasonable" waiting period (the waiting period does not erode the child's sense of motivation), the parent teaches the child to anticipate an upcoming pleasure, and the parent is viewed as trustworthy by the child.

Life is full of inevitable frustrations and waiting periods. Children must learn to accept them by relying on their inner motivation that provides the needed will to pursue their goals.

Academic motivation begins well before school starts. The family environment is the primary source of motivation with respect to intellectual activities. Before the age of 6, children are known to behave in a primarily verbal/motor fashion. However, they become intrigued when they see their parents doing something that they do not do, such as holding a book or a magazine for a long time. Children ask themselves, "What could be so interesting about something that you can't even play with?" Their growing curiosity about adult secrets and activities is the beginning of their motivation to read, among other things.

A Taste for Learning

Motivation is contagious. Children generally adhere to the same values as their parents because of the close relationship that exists between them. Children are also motivated to share in their parents' activities, initially by imitation and later by identification. According to a Danish study, 82% of six-to nine-year-old students with reading difficulties came from families who owned fewer than 10 books. If parents seldom read, if they do not lead intellectually challenging lives and do not involve themselves in their children's academic activities, then there is a strong chance that their children will not be interested either.

Many parents would like to magically inspire their children to be motivated in school. These parents may well be disappointed, because motivation comes from inside and cannot be forced. However, parents can play an encouraging role in this regard. To understand this, motivation can be compared to appetite. Children cannot be forced to have an appetite but can be encouraged to eat by varying meals and preparing tasty little dishes. In the same fashion, children cannot be forced to learn but may be encouraged to do so.

By comparing motivation to appetite, we can understand the strong environmental influence on learning activities. Let us consider the following situation, for example. A friend invites you for a meal. You are not very hungry but you accept the invitation just the same. You are very relaxed and content. Time passes quickly and your appetite increases. On the other hand, you may be very hungry before you eat but you completely lose your appetite because conflicts arise during the meal, and your stomach contracts.

Similarly, children's motivation for a particular activity will only grow if they enjoy doing it with the people around them. This greatly influences their motivation and the quality of what they learn.

Motivation Factors

Numerous studies have shown that other factors influence motivation. Children's concept of intelligence plays a role in their motivation. In today's society and schools, children who do well academically are viewed as intelligent. Unfortunately, many young people reverse the equation and associate poor academic performance with a lack of intelligence.

Many students have strong intellectual abilities but do not excel in school because of learning difficulties. Some make commendable efforts to improve their performance but, when unsuccessful, they downgrade themselves, feeling that they have disappointed the adults around them. It may also happen that these adults, noticing the children's fruitless efforts to improve, lead those children to believe (implicitly or explicitly) that they are not gifted intellectually.

To avoid this negative judgement that eats away at their self-esteem, many children simply lose interest in their studies. They are then said to be lazy, and if they only worked harder, they would do well. Children feel hurt less if they are considered lazy rather than unintelligent.

Children's motivation is also influenced by their concept of their learning objectives. We live in a society where performance, productivity, short-term efficiency and profitability are becoming increasingly important commodities. During their academic careers, children learn one way or another that "delivering the goods" is more important than worrying about how the goods are made. Children notice that efficiency and performance are encouraged, rather than effort and enjoyment. This realization diminishes their motivation to learn. They believe that to be considered a good or poor student depends on examination results, regardless of the energy and time devoted to their work in the preceding weeks. They also realize that evaluations play a large role, at the expense of the learning process itself. Their motivation diminishes because they feel obligated to produce a maximum amount of effort over a limited time to satisfy their parents, teachers and school administrators.

All learning must make sense. A person cannot be asked to perform an activity if its goal, usefulness, or value is not understood. To do otherwise insults intelligence and reduces motivation. Children must therefore be aware of the proven usefulness of what they are being asked to do. They will be much more motivated to learn linear measurements if they understand, for example, that this knowledge may be useful in carpentry or dressmaking. Children cannot always be expected to discover the relationship between knowledge and its use in everyday life by themselves. Sometimes we need to tell children about these relationships, which often give meaning or value to learning.

It is extremely important for parents to act as mediators between children and what they learn. The mediation must be in the form of continuous support, so that children understand the relationship between the principles of learning and elements of the real world. By talking to their parents, children can relate new information to what they already know. Similarly, adults can help children establish a connection between ideas or thoughts that they already possess with something that they have just learned.

Children are more motivated if they clearly understand the demands of a proposed activity. Some children overestimate the difficulty of tasks that they are asked to accomplish and lose their motivation because they are not confident they can overcome the challenge. Other children underestimate the complexity of particular activities and, judging them too easy or too dull, their motivation is weakened.

A realistic perception of an activity's challenges comes from an awareness of the desired objective, together with attitudes, stages and strategies necessary to attain it. Children must also be sure that they can rely on previously acquired skills and knowledge. Their motivation is directly linked to their perception of the feasibility of a given task or activity.

Setting Realistic Goals

One leitmotif that constantly recurs in education is that challenges in learning must be in line with children's abilities and adapted to their level and rate of development. Children are not happy if they fail due to unreasonably high goals or because the pace of teaching is too fast. They lose their motivation and feel worthless. A realistic goal is a judicious balance between tasks that are too difficult and too easy. For a goal to be realistic, it must match the following criteria:*

*Adapted from Sharp, Billy B., Claire Cox. *Choose Success: How to Set and Achieve All Your Goals*. New York: Hawthorn Books, 1970.

Conceivable: it must be possible to determine the goal clearly and distinguish the different stages for reaching it.

Believable: the goal must be linked to a personal value system, so a person can be sure that it can be achieved.

Attainable: the goal must be attainable using a person's own strengths, abilities and skills.

Controllable: the cooperation of another person must be available, if necessary.

Measurable: the goal must be measurable in terms of time and energy expended.

Desirable: a person must have the desire to achieve the goal.

Clear: the goal must be precise and unambiguous.

Constructive: the goal must allow for personal growth and be useful to others.

Children generally enjoy challenges. For them to be successful in their attempts, the goal suggested must be realistic, simple, and achievable within a short period of time and by using a process comprising various stages.

Learning to Learn

Everyone has their own way of learning and uses their own particular strategies for perceiving, processing and communicating information. Parents must help their children discover and choose ways to facilitate learning.

To elaborate further, let us compare the function of intelligence to a computer. First, information is entered, then processed and, finally, outputted. Several strategies can be used at each of these stages.

Children possess various tools for learning — perceptive, intellectual, neuromotor, etc. These abilities develop gradually and in stages. Children also have their own pace of learning, which must be recognized and respected. You cannot just teach any child any old thing at any old time — everything depends on the complexity of what is being learned and the child's methods of learning. For example, a six-year-old student cannot be asked to do numerical division, because he does not have the intellectual tools to perform such a task.

Some children are reminiscent of skilled workers who do not know how to use a new tool. They have the potential to do the work (that is, to learn), but they do not know how to go about it. Therefore, to achieve particular goals, children must learn to use their tools – i.e. select suitable learning strategies.

The Logical Equation of Learning

The result of motor, intellectual or social learning is a logical and causal process of attitudes and strategies that may be summarized in the following equation:

Too many students do not know that they can control their learning and their results. They often rely on external influences to explain their academic achievements. For example, a child will say that he/she gets good marks because the rest of the class is weak. Another child will blame failure in a particular subject on the fact that the teacher marked too severely.

True learning assumes that the logical connection between a beginning and an outcome are understood. Parents play an important role in this respect. They must help their children realize that no result (positive or negative) is magic; rather, it is the logical consequence of their attitudes (motivation, independence, responsibility) and the strategies that they have used.

Parents need to reassure their children by helping them realize that a negative outcome calls into question neither their personal value nor their intelligence, and that they can, to some extent, control their attitudes and strategies. Children need to know that they have not succeeded because they were not motivated enough or because they did not use the appropriate ways to succeed. If children want to succeed, they can and must modify their approach. This awareness will lead children to understand that success depends on positive attitudes and appropriate methods. Learning will then give children a feeling of efficiency and pride that will nourish their self-esteem.

Mistakes in the Learning Process

It is impossible to learn without making mistakes. Mistakes are inevitable and even necessary in a dynamic learning process. Children learn to learn in large part through their mistakes. Parents must therefore help their children be aware of their errors so that they can correct them and use ways to avoid repeating them. They will then learn to use other strategies. In finding new strategies to use, children must seek help from their parents, who may make suggestions but not impose their ideas.

Some parents believe that they are encouraging their children by telling them to "try harder." Many children find this concept too deep to grasp. In addition, this advice can be harmful because children may not have developed many learning strategies. In this case, what happens if children attempt to follow their parents' advice? They expend a great deal of energy and run a high risk of failure, because they are not using the correct methods. They then say that they tried harder and failed which, to them, indicates that they are unintelligent. Their self-esteem is thus undermined. To clarify this point, let us use an analogy. Let us suppose that you have never learned to swim. Your swimming instructor forces you to jump into four meters of water and just keeps telling you to try harder. What does this accomplish? Nothing, other than make you swallow a whole bunch of water! On the other hand, if the swimming instructor shows you how to keep your head above water and propel yourself forward, there is a good chance that his strategies combined with your efforts will succeed.

Children must accept errors in order to be aware of them. Too many children see their mistakes as failures. They then become perfectionists or refuse to participate in activities for fear of making more mistakes. Is this due to highly demanding parents or, perhaps more likely, to parents who cannot tolerate their own mistakes? Either way, children model themselves after their parents and see them as perfect beings because the parents never admit to making mistakes. Children feel obliged to be like their parents in order to be worthy of them. Parents should therefore be able to talk about their mistakes, so that their children realize that they too are allowed to make mistakes.

Accepting errors and learning from them is not an easy task in a society where, at work and at school, efficiency and profitability are important and mistakes are difficult to admit. Too often, children feel compelled to do what adults want them to do, and the adults emphasize outcomes at the expense of the learning process.

Teaching or Training Children?

The transition from theory to practice is sometimes difficult for children. Many are slow to relate the knowledge they acquire in school to its usefulness in everyday life. How can this phenomenon, which worries increasing numbers of parents and teachers, be explained? Above all, how can we help our children assimilate all the information available to them?

Young people are bombarded with all kinds of information, and many have difficulty connecting it all. This leads us to examine the nature of the teaching and training that our children receive to prepare them for the future. No studies have shown that today's youth are less adept than children in the past at establishing logical relationships between different ideas. However, everyone seems to agree that today's children are more informed than ever before. How then do we explain why so many children have this type of difficulty?

Parents Who Feel Powerless

People do not acquire most of their knowledge at school. Benjamin Bloom, a great American teacher, showed that people obtain about 80% of their knowledge outside the academic environment. When young children first go to nursery school, they have already acquired a great deal of knowledge, mostly due to their parents' teachings. Skills that are often quite complex, such as learning to speak, are acquired easily due in large part to the close relationships between parent and child. This relationship forms the basis of children's self-esteem. Perceiving that they are truly loved, children will conclude that they are lovable and valuable. Self-esteem is also known to be necessary in anticipating success, and it is also known that learning takes on a greater significance in the context of a close relationship.

Most parents know how to guide the learning of preschool children, but there are some who feel less competent or unable to support their children's endeavours in school.

In school, it is teachers who initiate the learning process, not parents. Being unable to share in their children's in-class motivation, experimentation, and learning process as a whole, some parents feel as if they have nothing more to do with the process. They feel even more excluded from the academic process if they do not understand the programs and the new teaching methods. They feel powerless to help their children learn.

Children develop in many ways; however, in the academic arena, parents soon find that learning is divided into a series of objectives for each subject. Many feel completely lost in this respect. In addition, unlike their first years of life, children must absorb all this knowledge and ability in a time frame determined by examination deadlines. If a child cannot walk by the age of one, that child is not made to repeat that first year. However, it is a different story if a child is not able to do simple arithmetic (e.g. 2 + 2) at the end of the first year of school. School curricula are rarely synchronized with a child's pace of development.

Ties to "Real Life"

Before school age, children learn things that are basically linked to their immediate needs, and their skills and knowledge are regularly put to use in their environment. At school, they are made to learn things that seem strange, even remote from their daily lives. For example, children do not immediately see the point of subtraction with borrowing. Like adults, children are not motivated to complete a task if they do not understand its usefulness. Parents have an important role to play in this respect. They must show children how to make the connection between things learned in school and their possible application in "real life." This attitude is essential for encouraging children's motivation and helping them apply their knowledge in different areas.

A single isolated piece of information is useless to children if they cannot relate it to knowledge they have already acquired. Pieces of knowledge become elements of training when children are capable of immediately linking them with analogies, similarities and logical relations, allowing connections to be made. Conversations during mealtimes, for example, are ideal times to make these connections. For example, say your child has just learned that Christopher Columbus discovered the Americas. While discussing this with your child, you could explain that Christopher Columbus first landed in the Dominican Republic, where his aunt went on vacation last year, that Colombia is a South American country named after this explorer, etc. There is an excellent chance that your child will always remember the part that Christopher Columbus played in the history of the American continent. A television program and a drive in the car are also good opportunities to help children establish these kinds of relationships.

A School System in Crisis

The school system is currently in the midst of a crisis with respect to organization, function and purpose. This has led to an alarming increase in the school dropout rate. This disastrous phenomenon provides an opportunity to examine certain accepted facts. Organizational factors appear to encourage the acquisition of knowledge in a piecemeal fashion, with pieces of information being isolated from one another.

In primary school, students participate in many programs, each developed independently of the other. The teachers of each subject must satisfy a great number of different learning objectives. This division was based on the logic of the subject matter, which does not always match the logic of students' development. Learning objectives are organized in a sequential, linear fashion, and students often have difficulty making the connection.

Each program stands alone, and is designed to facilitate the acquisition of skills and knowledge that are often not related to the objectives of the other programs. Each program has its own internal vertical logic, but there is little horizontal logic between subjects. Children do not have one type of intelligence for learning English and another for mathematics. They have an overall knowledge base and transfer intellectual skills from one area to another. However, for children to do this, school programs must be developed in a way that encourages these connections to be made. Unfortunately, the teaching vocation seems to be made up of separate compartments. Therefore, it is hardly surprising that students find it difficult to connect the ideas taught in the various programs.

Bringing Meaning to Teaching

Children can only assimilate new knowledge based on what they already know. The fundamental difference between the student who learns easily and the one who experiences difficulties lies in the ability to relate old and new knowledge. Some teachers do not devote enough time or energy to encourage students to establish relationships between ideas and to integrate them in a way that is conducive to other learning. Discovering these new relationships often motivates children.

Teachers and parents alike must help children understand the usefulness of each piece of knowledge without having to worry about report card marks. Academic knowledge is only useful in terms of its application to an actual activity, whether in the present or the future.

The elimination of piecemeal learning and learning objectives is under consideration in certain educational institutions, an innovative and laudable step.

Integrating various subjects allows knowledge to endure over time and also enables children to apply this knowledge generally and personally, opening up the scientific and artistic discoveries of the world in which we live.

Encouraging a Sense of Responsibility

Many children have difficulty taking responsibility for their school work. The ability to be solely responsible in this area does not magically appear once a child enters secondary school. It is part of a continuous process instilled in children from early childhood.

Like socialization, children gradually develop the ability to be responsible and independent, with sudden leaps forward and temporary setbacks. The sense of responsibility varies according to children's activities. A child can be responsible when it comes to tidying up a bedroom, but much less so when schoolwork is involved.

It goes without saying that children's responsibilities must suit their particular level of development. Before starting school, children should already be taking on some small responsibilities, such as tying shoes, tidying up toys, etc.

However, it is important to note that a sense of responsibility has nothing to do with blind obedience or routine. Parents must help their children understand the sense of value and trustworthiness that having responsibilities brings.

Children cannot be expected to immediately assume responsibility for schoolwork if they have not already learned to carry out small tasks around the house.

School Responsibilities

School responsibilities are generally the first type of responsibility that children must assume outside the family. Some are less prepared than others for this situation. Taking responsibility for schoolwork necessarily involves motivation and independence, and becoming a responsible student requires a personal investment and the ability to maintain this course of action.

Here we will review some elements of motivation and independence, clarifying their roles in the development of academic responsibility.

Motivation has been defined as the anticipation of pleasure during an activity or the anticipation of the activity's usefulness. It is comprised of children's inner drive and energy, independence and commitment. Children willingly put time and effort into a school activity when they are convinced it could be enjoyable or useful.

Appearing well before the beginning of school, motivation is directly influenced by family values. Parents who are involved in few intellectual activities (reading, writing, etc.) will have difficulty encouraging their children to participate in such activities. However, when children are assigned homework, parents must still help them to understand its purpose and take responsibility. If this is not done, children will balk at doing the homework because they do not understand its purpose. It will then be seen as an adult demand and a source of frustration.

The ability to make choices and accept the consequences, whether positive or negative, is the basis of independence. This skill is fundamental to the learning process and does not appear suddenly or by magic. Making choices involves risk and, above all, giving up certain things. This constraint is often a source of ambivalence, even among adults. Independence is essential if a student is to assume responsibility; in fact, it implies that the student has already decided to engage in school activities.

Mistakes are inevitable and necessary in learning. They allow children to adjust their strategies and find new ways to reach goals. Mistakes also give children a chance to evaluate themselves, correct their strategies and think about the choices they have made.

It is important to help children become aware of their mistakes. This helps the children learn not to repeat them. In addition, the corrections and adjustments required stimulate mental flexibility and adaptability.

Becoming a Responsible Student

Children's sense of academic responsibility is indistinguishable from their motivation and independence. This is evidenced by children's hard work. To keep up with schoolwork, they must continually invest their energy in motivation and take risks in choosing methods and strategies.

To become responsible students, children must also gradually develop their own way of working. In the case of homework or an exam to study for, the planning and method of work must include the following:

- anticipate the steps for doing homework or studying for an exam;
- anticipate the time required for each stage in order to meet the deadline;
- anticipate the methods or strategies to be used in each stage;
- anticipate a method of self-evaluation for reaching goals.

Lastly, it should be remembered that each time adults do something that children could have done by themselves, the latter's independence and sense of responsibility are harmed.

Signs That Children Have a Sense of Competency

Children with a well-established sense of competency will demonstrate most of the following:

- Remember past successes
- Anticipate enjoyment of an activity
- Understand the importance of suggested activities or learning
- Feel proud upon succeeding
- Show interest in learning more
- Show intellectual curiosity
- Demonstrate ability to choose between different strategies or methods
- Demonstrate ability to persevere despite challenge
- Show creativity
- Take initiative and calculated risks
- Demonstrate ability to re-apply and generalize skills and knowledge
- Show ability to recognize and accept errors
- Remain relaxed while learning

Parental Attitudes That Encourage a Sense of Competency in Children

Parents may adopt a wide range of attitudes to encourage a feeling of competency in their children:

- Understand their children's abilities and level of development
- Help their children remember past successes
- Suggest stimulating, enjoyable activities
- Tell their children about the usefulness of activities or learning
- Suggest realistic goals that match their children's abilities
- Respect their children's pace of learning
- Foster their children's independence
- Encourage a sense of responsibility in their children
- Regularly review goals to help their children understand the connection between their attitudes and strategies and subsequent results
- Suggest different strategies and ways of learning
- Help their children recognize, minimize and accept mistakes
- Help their children correct their mistakes
- Encourage their children's creativity
- Help their children avoid performance anxiety

- Emphasize the importance of learning
- Focus on their children's good strategies and responses with positive feedback
- Respect their children's individual pace of learning
- Stimulate their children's thought development

Conclusion

▼

Research and published works confirm that self-esteem is the principal factor in preventing adjustment and learning difficulties in children, as well as depression and mental illness in adults. Therefore, it could reasonably be said that self-esteem is a passport for life.

Every human being possesses the strength and resources to overcome life's challenges and difficulties. However, to accomplish this, we must recognize our ability to face these challenges. The word "esteem," which comes from the Latin "estimare," means "to determine the value of" and "to have an opinion of." In everyday language, "self-esteem" means "to determine one's self-worth or personal value." However, to determine our value, we must first be aware of it. Parents and adults play a major role in the awareness of self-worth that every child achieves.

As a rule, every child has great value in the eye of his/her parents. Unfortunately, children do not always realize this. Far too many children who display great qualities and who seem to have no difficulty learning or adjusting do not realize their own value, or belittle themselves. This is because of a lack of positive reinforcement on the part of the parents and educators who are important in the children's lives.

These adults must first help children recognize their own particular characteristics (abilities, qualities, etc.) and establish their own identity. Every child needs a passport that confers a positive identity on them. This passport is given to them by their parents, who act in some respects like a country to its citizens. With this passport, children can make their way through life in total confidence.

Self-esteem does not come from a simple awareness of one's own strengths, qualities and talents. It also assumes an accurate perception of one's difficulties and limitations. Adults must help children be aware of their difficulties and view them as challenges that they can overcome. Belief in children's abilities instills feelings of confidence and optimism. Parents and educators must also support children in their search for ways to overcome challenges.

Self-esteem is a complex and changeable process that is not limited to *liking* or *not liking* oneself. Popular opinion often confuses the terms "overestimate," "underestimate" and "estimate." When we overestimate ourselves, we have a high opinion of ourselves without realizing our difficulties or limitations; it is an omnipotent or narcissistic feeling. When we underestimate or belittle ourselves without thinking about our strengths or qualities, we restrict ourselves to feelings of depression. Self-esteem is a healthy and realistic feeling, which changes constantly and even falters at times. Self-esteem lies somewhere between narcissism and depression.

Self-esteem is the most valuable gift parents can give their children. This gift is only made possible by forming close, loving relationships. Children who have a strong physical and psychological sense of security, who feel confident when faced with life, know themselves and their own identity, who feel a strong sense of belonging to their family and to a group, who develop abilities and are ultimately aware of their own personal value, have received a great gift on which they can rely throughout their lives when faced with challenges. This is the best passport that children can possess, allowing them to develop fully and grow continually.

References

ANDRÉ, CHRISTOPHE and FRANÇOIS LELORD. *L'estime de soi: s'aimer pour mieux vivre avec les autres*. Paris: Odile Jacob, 1999. 288 p.

DUCLOS, GERMAIN, DAMNIELLE LAPORTE and JACQUES ROSS. *L'estime de soi de nos adolescents: guide pratique à l'intention des parents*. Montreal: Les éditions de l'Hôpital Sainte-Justine, 1995. 178 p.

DUCLOS, GERMAIN, DAMNIELLE LAPORTE and JACQUES ROSS. *Les besoins et les défis des enfants de 6 à 12 ans : vivre en harmonie avec des apprentis sorciers*. Saint Lambert, Quebec: Les éditions Héritage, 1994. 367 p.

Estime de soi : lettres au parents 1994-1998. Comité estime de soi, Module famille-enfance-jeunesse, CLSC La Presqu'île. Vaudreuil-Dorion: CLSC La Presqu'île, 1998. Not paginated.

LAPORTE, DANIELLE and LISE SÉVIGNY. *Comment développer l'estime de soi de nos enfants : guide pratique à l'intention des parents d'enfants de 6 à 12 ans*. New, revised, enlarged edition. Montreal: Les éditions de l'Hôpital Sainte-Justine, 1998. 119 p.

LAPORTE, DANIELLE. *Pour favoriser l'estime de soi des tout-petits : guide pratique à l'intention des parents d'enfants de 0 à 6 ans*. Montreal: Les éditions de l'Hôpital Sainte-Justine, 1997. 127 p.

MONBOURQUETTE, JEAN, MYRNA LADOUCEUR and JACQUELINE DESJARDINS-PROULX. *Je suis aimable, je suis capable : parcours pour l'estime et l'affirmation de soi*. New edition. Outremont, Quebec: Novalis, 1998. 362 p.

PARENTING

A Practical Guide to Learning Disabilities

Denise Destrempes-Marquez and Louise Lafleur
ISBN 2-921858-92-4
2001
120 pages

Some 10 to 15 percent of the population lives with learning disabilities. These disabilities are not due to a low IQ, but rather to difficulties acquiring and processing information. Imagine the frustration of children with learning disabilities who are unable to keep up with their classmates. Think of their parents who do not understand the situation or know what to do. This guide provides parents with basic information on learning disabilities and on practical ways of taking effective action.

Scoliosis Surgery
How to Get Prepared

Julie Joncas
ISBN 2-921858-82-7
2000
96 pages

This book is intended for adolescents awaiting scoliosis corrective surgery and their families. Using a simple and lively writing style, the author (and her collaborators from Quebec and France) explain in detail the condition of scoliosis its corrective surgery. This reference provides readers with complete information about the periods before, during after surgery, and helps reduce the associated with this type of surgery.

Self-Esteem:
A Passport for life

Germain Duclos
ISBN 2-921858-93-2
2001
114 pages

A child's self-esteem must from a very early age by his or and educators. In this book describes how to pass on to elements of self-esteem — knowledge, the sense of group and competency. forward language, the a itive educational attitude better acknowledge the